Enjoy Your Business Trip

I Talk You Talk Press

Copyright © 2018 I Talk You Talk Press

ISBN: 978-4-909733-19-1

www.italkyoutalk.com

info@italkyoutalk.com

All rights reserved. No part of this publication may be resold, reproduced, stored in retrieval system, copied in any form or by any means, electronic, mechanical, photocopying, recording or otherwise transmitted without the prior written permission from the publisher. You must not circulate this publication in any format, online or otherwise.

This is a work of fiction. Names, characters, businesses, organizations, products, places, events and incidents are either the products of the author's imagination or are used in a fictitious manner. We have no affiliation with any existing companies mentioned in this story. Any resemblance to actual persons, living or dead, existing stories or actual events is purely coincidental.

Although the author and publisher have made every effort to ensure that the contents of this book were correct at press time, the author and publisher do not assume and hereby disclaim any liability to any party for any loss, damage, or disruption caused by errors or omissions, whether such errors or omissions result from negligence, accident, or any other cause.

For more information, see the Copyright Notice on our website.

Image copyright: © Anatoly Repin - Fotolia.com #61064016 Standard License

CONTENTS

Introduction	1
Format of this book	2
1. Before you go	3
2. Travel	5
3. Check in	8
COFFEE BREAK	10
4. Calling the office	11
5. Arriving at the office and introductions	14
6. Presentations	16
COFFEE BREAK	18
7. Meetings	19
8. Eating and drinking	21
9. Saying goodbye	24

COFFEE BREAK	26
10. Check out	27
Thank You	29
About the Author	31

INTRODUCTION

So, you are going on an international business trip! Of course, you must be very excited. You will have the chance to experience office life in another country, and use your English. You will have the chance to meet new people, and to learn about their business culture. It will help you in your future career.

But perhaps you are also a little nervous. Perhaps you are worried about travelling to your destination, or making travel plans. Perhaps you are worried about giving a presentation, or participating in meetings in English. Will you be able to express yourself? Will you be able to communicate smoothly? If you are worried about these things, this book is for you.

In this book we give you advice, and many example sentences, conversations, words and phrases to help you communicate and make your business trip a success.

If you practice hard, you will be able to have a conversation, give an opinion, make a presentation, talk about new ideas, and talk about things that are a problem for you.

FORMAT OF THIS BOOK

Each unit starts with a question and an answer section. The questions are real questions from our adult students going on business trips.

The next section has sample sentences and sample conversations to give you the tools you need to communicate smoothly.

There are also "coffee break" columns with real life stories from people we know who travel overseas on business.

We hope this book is useful to you, and we hope you have a wonderful business trip!

1. BEFORE YOU GO

Q: Should I contact the overseas office before I go?
Advice: If it is your first time to go to the office, or your first time to contact or speak to the people in the office, it is a good idea to send an email before you go. You can ask questions and it might make you feel less nervous. You will "break the ice". ("Break the ice" means "get to know someone".)

Example emails

1. Attending a meeting

---Dear Ms Baker,
This is Roberto Angeli, the business development manager from the Rome office. I understand that you are in charge of the general meeting. As you know, I am coming to take part in the meeting. I will be in the company offices from 1st - 5th September. I have prepared all the documents for my presentation in the session on the 2nd. Is there anything else I should prepare?

I will arrive in Sydney at 4:30pm on 31st August. I will call you to let you know I have arrived.

I am looking forward to meeting you and everyone in the Sydney office.

Best regards,
Roberto Angeli ---

2. Going to work with someone you contact often and with whom

you have become friendly.

---Dear James,
I am coming to the Chicago office for a week! I hope it will be enough time for us to finish the plans for the new project. It will be great to finally meet you after so many months exchanging emails.
I will email you all the work I have done before I leave. Can you send me any new ideas you have? I will have time on the plane to look at them.
I'm arriving in Chicago on Sunday, May 9th and I've made a reservation at the Hotel O'Hare. From Google Maps it seems like this is near your offices.
I'll come to the office around 10 am on Monday, May 10th.
Looking forward to seeing you and working with you,
Regards,
Michel---

3. Going to visit another office.

---Dear Mr Monkton,

My name is Angela Lau. I have been appointed as the manager for the new branch office in Hong Kong. Mr Furlong, the Manager for Apex International, suggested that I spend some time in one of the other branch offices.
He suggested your office in Bristol and I believe he has contacted you about my visit.
I want to learn as much as possible about how you run your office, so I am very grateful for the opportunity.
I'm looking forward to meeting you and your colleagues.

Yours sincerely,
Angela Lau---

Q. Should I take gifts?
Advice: If someone in the office has helped you a lot, for example, making hotel reservations or local travel arrangements, it might be nice to take them a small gift, such as a box of sweets.
Perhaps if you have been working with someone a lot and you have become email friends you could take a gift either for them or for their children.

2. TRAVEL

Q: No one will meet me at the airport. I have to go to the hotel by myself. How can I get information in the airport about trains, buses or taxis?

Advice: There will be signs for "ground transportation" in the airport. But if you don't know where to go, look for the information desk. Here are some useful phrases for asking about ground transportation.

Example Sentences:
1) What is the cheapest/fastest/best way to get to the city centre please?
2) Could you tell me how to get to the city centre please?
3) Where do the buses/trains leave from?
4) Where can I buy a ticket for the bus/train?
5) How much is it from the airport to the city centre by bus/train/taxi?
6) I have a reservation at ABC Hotel. Is there a shuttle bus or courtesy bus to that hotel?

Example Conversations at the Airport:
1)
Roberto: Excuse me, what is the fastest way to get to the city centre please?
Information desk staff: The train is the fastest. Just follow the signs to the station.

Roberto: How long does it take to get to the centre?
Information desk staff: Not long. Only about fifteen minutes.
Roberto: OK, thank you.

2)
Michel: Could you tell me how to get to the city centre please?
Information desk staff: You could take a taxi, but it would be much cheaper to take a train.
Michel: I see. Where can I buy a train ticket?
Information desk staff: You can buy a ticket in the station.
Michel: OK, thank you.

Here are some questions you might need to ask the driver if you are taking the bus.

7) Do I pay you now, or when I get off?
8) How much is it to the city centre?
9) Do you go to the station area?
10) How long will it take to get to the city centre?
11) I'm staying at ABC Hotel. Which stop should I get off at?

Here are some sentences you can use if you are taking a taxi*.

12) How much is the fare to ABC Hotel?
13) How long will it take to get to the hotel?
14) To ABC Hotel please.
15) How long will it take to get to the city centre?

In some countries, it is usual to give a tip to the taxi driver. Check this before you go.

Here are some sentences you can use if you are taking the train.

16) A one-way/single* ticket to Central Station please.
17) Which platform does the train leave from?
18) What time does the train leave?
19) Is it an express train?
20) When is the next train?
21) Could I have a reserved seat?

22) Do I need to reserve a seat?

One-way ticket is American English. Single ticket is British English.

Q: I might need to change my return flight to a later date. Can you give me some sentences?

Advice: If you have to change your flight, a receptionist or secretary at the office might do it for you. Here are some sentences you can use to ask for help.

23) I have to change my flight. Could you help me?
24) I haven't finished the work I need to do here in the office. I am going to stay a little longer. Can you help me change my return flight?
25) How can I change my travel arrangements?

Example Conversation:

Roberto: Ms Baker has asked me to stay for two extra days. I have to change my flight. Could you help me please?
Rebecca: Sure, do you want me to check what flights are available?
Roberto: Yes, please. If you don't mind.
Rebecca: No problem. Leave your tickets with me.
Roberto: OK, thank you.

Here are some sentences you can use when you call the airline.

26) Hello, I'd like to change my flight to a later date.
27) Do you have any seats available for the eighth of September?
28) Will there be an extra charge for this change?
29) Do you have any seats available on another flight?
30) Do you have a flight leaving on the evening of the sixth of September?
31) Can I change my flight online?

3. CHECK IN

Q. I want to ask the hotel staff for advice on how to get to the office, and how to get around town. Can you give me some sentences?

Advice: The hotel staff will be able to help you with directions. They can also help you find a place to eat, and give you advice about the local area. They usually have maps, and will mark places on them for you.

First, let's check in. Here are some sentences and questions you can use when checking in.

1) I have a reservation. My name is Angela Lau.
2) I am staying for five nights.
3) Is breakfast included?
4) What time is breakfast served?
5) Could you give me a wake-up call at six am please?
6) Here is my passport.

Here are some more sentences and questions you can use to ask about the local area.

7) Do you have a map of the local area?
8) Are there any restaurants nearby?
9) How far is it from here to Green Street?
10) Can I walk there? Or do I need to take a taxi?

Example Conversations in the Hotel:

1)
Angela: Hello. I have a reservation. My name is Angela Lau.
Hotel staff: Hello Ms Lau. You are staying with us for five nights, is that right?
Angela: Yes, that's right.
Hotel staff: Could you fill in this form please?
Angela: Sure.

2)
Michel: Is breakfast included?
Hotel staff: Yes it is. It is served in the first floor restaurant between six am and nine am.
Michel: OK, that's great. Could you give me a wake-up call at six am please?
Hotel staff: Of course. Here is your key. Your room is on the seventh floor. The elevators are to your right.
Michel: OK, thank you very much.

3)
Angela: Excuse me, do you have a map of the local area?
Hotel staff: Sure. Here is a map. I'll mark the hotel on it for you.
Angela: Thanks. Are there any restaurants nearby?
Hotel staff: There are many in the street behind the hotel. The hotel also has a nice restaurant that serves lunch and dinner.
Angela: OK, thank you very much. Tomorrow morning I have to be at Green Street for nine am. How far is it from here to Green Street?
Hotel staff: Not so far.
Angela: Can I walk there, or do I need to take a taxi?
Hotel staff: You can walk there in ten minutes.
Angela: Could you please mark it on the map for me?
Hotel staff: Sure.

COFFEE BREAK

"Before I go on a business trip, I research everything very carefully. I look for the office on Google Maps, I search the best ways to get from the airport to the hotel, and I check the average taxi fares, so I know how much to pay. I also look at the office homepage. My company has staff profiles on the homepage of each office, so I read about the people before I meet them. This helps me to start conversations with people when I get to the office."

Mr M.H. (36) Visits the USA and Canada frequently

"I got lost on my first day going to the office! The hotel staff recommended I take a taxi, but it was a beautiful sunny day, so I decided to walk. I tried to follow the map, but I took a wrong turn. I went into a coffee shop and asked 'Excuse me, could you tell me how to get to....?' The man in the shop gave me directions, but he said, 'You are very far from there. It will take about fifteen minutes!' I looked for a taxi on the road, but there weren't any, so I ran through the streets and found the office at last. I was ten minutes late! Luckily, everyone was very nice and understanding. Next time, I'll take a taxi, even if the weather is nice!"

Mr T.K. (25) Visited Australia

4. CALLING THE OFFICE

Q. I have to call the office when I arrive. I'm nervous about using the telephone in English. What should I do if I can't understand the other person?

Advice: Many people feel nervous when they make a phone call in a foreign language. Speak slowly and clearly, and if you don't understand, politely ask the other person to slow down. Most people will speak slowly and clearly to help you understand.

Here are some sentences you can use when making a phone call.
1) Hello. This is Roberto Angeli from the Rome office.
2) Could I speak to Ms Baker please?
3) I am calling to tell you that I have arrived in Sydney.
4) I'm looking forward to meeting everyone tomorrow.
5) I'm sorry. I didn't catch that. Could you say that again please?
6) I'm sorry. I don't understand. Could you speak more slowly please?

Example Conversation on the Phone:
1)
Roberto: Hello. This is Roberto Angeli from the Rome office.
Receptionist: Hello, Mr Angeli.
Roberto: Could I speak to Ms Baker please?
Receptionist: Just a moment please. I'll put you through.
....

Ms Baker: This is Karen Baker speaking.

Roberto: Hello, Ms Baker. This is Roberto Angeli from the Rome office. I am calling to tell you that I have arrived in Sydney.

Ms Baker: Welcome to Sydney! I'm glad you arrived safely. How was your trip?

Roberto: I'm sorry. I didn't catch that. Could you say that again please?

Ms Baker: How was your trip? Was your flight OK?

Roberto: Oh, it was fine thank you. I'm looking forward to meeting you and your staff tomorrow.

Ms Baker: We are looking forward to meeting you too. See you at 9 am tomorrow.

Roberto: Yes, see you then. Bye.

Q. What do I say if the person I want to speak to is not there? Should I leave a message?

Advice: You can leave a message, or call back later. Here are some phrases you can use.

7) Could I leave a message?
8) Could you please tell Ms Baker that I called?
9) Could you please tell Ms Baker that I arrived in Sydney?
10) What time will she be back/free?
11) I will call back later.
12) I will call back at five pm.

Example Conversations:
1)
Receptionist: ABC Holdings, Rebecca speaking.

Roberto: This is Roberto Angeli from the Rome office. Could I speak to Ms Baker please?

Rebecca: I'm afraid Ms Baker is in a meeting at the moment. Could I take a message?

Roberto: Could you please tell her that I called? I have arrived in Sydney. I will call back later. What time will her meeting finish?

Rebecca: It should finish around five pm.

Roberto: OK, I'll call back then. Thank you.

Rebecca: OK, thanks for calling. Bye.

Roberto: Bye.

2)
Secretary: Mr Monkton's office. Stanley Jones speaking.
Angela: This is Angela Lau. I would like to speak to Mr Monkton please.
Stanley: I'm afraid Mr Monkton is in a meeting at the moment.
Angela: Could you please tell him that I called? I have arrived in Bristol. I will call back later. What time will his meeting finish?
Stanley: It should finish around five pm.
Angela: OK, I'll call back then. Thank you.
Stanley: I will give you Mr Monkton's direct telephone number. Either Mr Monkton will answer, or I will. That will be easier for you.

Here is another example. This time, the receptionist offers to call Roberto back.

Receptionist: ABC Holdings, Rebecca speaking.
Roberto: This is Roberto Angeli from the Rome office. Could I speak to Ms Baker please?
Rebecca: I'm afraid Ms Baker is on another line at the moment.
Roberto: On another line? I'm sorry, I don't understand.
Rebecca: She's on another telephone. She is talking to another person.
Roberto: Oh, I see.
Rebecca: I will ask her to call you back when she has finished. Could I have your number, Mr Angeli?
Roberto: Yes. It's 0123, 456, 789.
Rebecca: Thank you. I'll ask her to call you back when she has finished her call.
Roberto: OK, thank you. Bye.
Rebecca: OK, thanks for calling. Bye.

5. ARRIVING AT THE OFFICE AND INTRODUCTIONS

Q. When I meet people in the office, should I use Mr/Ms and last name, or should I use their first names?
Advice: When meeting people for the first time, it is better to use Mr/Ms and "last name" until they tell you to use their first name. Or, you can ask them directly which name you should use.

Many students think that people in English speaking countries use first names only, but this is not true. It depends on the situation. For example, if you are a school student, you never call a teacher by his or her first name, unless the teacher tells you to. If you don't know a person well, you should use Mr/Ms + "last name" until the person says "please call me (first name)." Then, it is OK to use first names. (You can use children's first names from the beginning.)

At reception
1) Good morning. I'm Roberto Angeli from the Rome office. I'm here for a meeting.
2) I'm here for a meeting with Ms Baker.
3) I'm here to attend the general meeting.

Meeting the people in the office
4) I'm Roberto Angeli from the Rome office.
5) Nice to meet you.
6) How do you do?*

7) Please call me Roberto.
8) What should I call you?

* Be careful! How do you do?

"How do you do?" does not mean "How are you?" It means "Nice to meet you". It is not a question!

Example Conversation. In the Office

1)
Roberto: Hello. I'm Roberto Angeli from the Rome office.
Ms Baker: Nice to meet you, Mr Angeli. I'm Karen Baker.
Roberto: How do you do Ms Baker?
Ms Baker: Please call me Karen.
Roberto: Thank you Karen. Please call me Roberto.
Karen: Let me introduce you to our sales manager Tom.

2)
James: Terry, this is Michel from the Paris office. He is here to work with me for a few days.
Terry: Hi Michel. James has talked about you. Nice to meet you.
Roberto: Nice to meet you too.
Terry: How was your trip?
Roberto: It was long, but it was fine. And I slept well last night.
Terry: That's good. I hope you and James make a lot of progress.

Q: Should I shake hands?

Advice: It depends which country you are visiting. If you are in an English-speaking country, you should shake hands. Use your right hand.

This is a normal custom, especially for men. When you shake hands, grip the other person's hand firmly (but not too firmly!) Many women shake hands too.

6. PRESENTATIONS

Q. This is my first time to give a presentation in English. I am worried that people will not understand my English. I'm also worried that people will ask me questions that I don't understand.

Advice: Of course, you will have planned your presentation very carefully and practiced a lot before you arrive, so don't worry too much. Speak slowly and clearly. Use short sentences. If you can, use PowerPoint or other slides to help you to communicate your message. Prepare some documents with the important information on them so people can read too. These documents are called "handouts". Some people may ask questions. If you don't understand the question, it is OK to say, "I'm sorry. I didn't understand. Could you say that again?" Or "I'm sorry, could you repeat that please?"

Example Sentences before your Presentation:
1) I need to photocopy these handouts.
2) Can you show me how to use the photocopier please?
3) Where can I set up my computer?
4) Can you help me set up my computer/the projector?

Example Sentences for your Presentation:
1) It's a pleasure to be here today to talk to you about…
2) Today I'm going to talk about…
3) I'm going to talk about the situation in…
4) First, I'd like to give you some information about…

5) Please look at page one of your handouts.
6) This slide shows…
7) This diagram shows…
8) As you can see…
9) I'd like to finish by saying that…
10) If you have any questions, I'd be happy to answer them.

Example Presentation:

Roberto: Good morning everyone. I'm Roberto Angeli from the Rome office. Today I'm going to talk about the sales data for Italy. First, I'd like to give you some information about the situation in the Rome office. Please look at sheet one of your handouts. This shows the structure of the office and the roles of each staff member.

There are twenty of us in the office. We are responsible for all of Italy.

Please look at this slide. This graph shows the sales figures for the past two years. As you can see, sales have increased by twenty percent over the past year…

I'd like to finish by saying that we are on target to reach three million euros in sales by the end of next year. This slide shows our targets and our progress.

If you have any questions, I'd be happy to answer them.

Example Sentences when Answering Questions:
1) That's a very good question.
2) The data is on page five of the handouts.
3) I'm sorry, I don't have that data with me, but I can send it to you by email when I return to Rome.
4) I'm sorry. I'm not sure what you want to know. Can you explain a little more?
5) If we go back to one of my previous slides, I will be able to show you the answer to your question.

COFFEE BREAK

"When I went to Japan, I had to give a presentation in English. My native language is Spanish, and I don't speak any Japanese. To help me, I made lots of handouts. I used many pictures and diagrams in my PowerPoint slides too. My presentation was very visual, and I think it was easy to understand. This made me less nervous about my English and about communicating. Everyone seemed to understand, so they asked very few questions. My advice to other people giving presentations in a foreign language is 'make it visual!'"
Ms R.S. (45) Visited Japan

"In my country, we don't shake hands when we meet. We bow. So when I visit America on business, I feel nervous about shaking hands. Should I grip the hand lightly? Should I grip the hand firmly? My English teacher tells me I should grip the hand firmly, but not too firmly. Should I shake hands with women also? I notice some women don't shake hands. I visit the American office of our company many times, and the last time I visited, one of the men gave me a hug! I was so shocked! Maybe he feels friendly towards me!"
Mr T.K. (25) Visits the USA frequently for business

7. MEETINGS

Q. I have to attend a meeting while I am on my trip. I want to give my opinions, but I don't want to say anything rude. Can you give me some phrases I can use when agreeing and disagreeing?

Advice: It is important to be polite when you give your opinions, or when you want to confirm someone else's opinion. Here are some phrases you can use.

Example Sentences:
1) Excuse me for interrupting, but do you mean…?
2) I think it is a good idea, but how about…?
3) I agree with Paula. I think we should…
4) I think it is a good idea, but we should think carefully about…
5) I'm not sure that would work very well in my country because…
6) I'm afraid I don't agree because…
7) I understand your point, but I think it would be better to…
8) I don't think that is a problem for our office.
9) I'm not sure about that.
10) I'd just like to say that…

Example Conversation:
Karen: OK, let's discuss marketing strategies. I'd like to hear all of your opinions. Tom, do you have any ideas?

Tom: I think we need to focus more on social media. Our

campaign on Twitter worked very well last year, I think it would be good to roll that out across other platforms, like Facebook, and…

Roberto: Excuse me for interrupting, but does 'roll out' mean 'introduce'?

Tom: Yes, I guess so. We should introduce more campaigns.

Roberto: I think it is a good idea, but how about having more in-store campaigns? We had a successful campaign a few months ago. Sales really improved.

Tom: I'm not sure that would work very well over here. We tried an in-store campaign in Melbourne, but we didn't see such good results.

Karen: That's true, but we could try again. But we should think carefully about how to set up the campaign. I think there were many problems in the setup last time.

Roberto: I agree that the setup is very important. We spent around six months planning our in-store campaign. How about a joint campaign in-store and on social media?

Tom: At the same time?

Roberto: Yes. I think that would attract attention and it wouldn't be so difficult to setup.

Tom: I'm afraid I don't agree, because we have a staff shortage in our office at the moment. I think it would be difficult to set up.

Roberto: I understand your point, but maybe the Rome office could help you. We have a lot of people in the office.

....

Karen: OK, I think that is all. Would anyone like to add anything else?

Tom: No, I think we have covered everything.

Karen: Roberto? Would you like to add anything?

Roberto: I'd just like to say that it has been very interesting to hear about the situation over here, and the strategies you are using. It has given me some ideas, so thank you.

Karen: Thank you. Your information has been very useful to us too. OK, let's leave it there. Tom, could you write up the main points of the meeting before Roberto leaves?

Tom: Sure, I'll do it today.

8. EATING AND DRINKING

Q: I want to go out for dinner or drinks with the people in the office. How can I invite them out?

Advice: It depends on the country and also the actual company. In some countries they will probably invite you to dinner, or drinks. They may have planned a small party for you and any other visitors. In other countries the person you are working most closely with might invite you to have lunch or a meal after work.

Example Sentences: Inviting

1) Do the people in the office go out on Fridays for drinks after work? I'd like to meet some other people in the office.

2) The proposal you made in the meeting today was very interesting. Do you have time to go out for a drink so we could discuss it some more?

3) You have been very helpful. I leave tomorrow, so I am wondering if I could take you out for lunch today.

4) You guys have helped me so much. Can I buy you a drink after work?

5) I'm thinking of going for a few drinks tonight. Would you like to join me?

Example Sentences: Accepting invitations

6) Thank you! I'd love to join you.

7) Thanks for the invitation. I'd like to go out with you.

8) It's kind of you to invite me, but I have to practise my

presentation tonight. Could we go tomorrow instead?

9) That's great. I'd like to meet some other people from the office.

10) Thank you, Mr Monkton. I will be happy to join you and your wife for dinner.

Example Sentences: Asking people where to eat or drink
You can ask people about places to eat and drink.

11) Are there any good restaurants or bars near here?

12) I want to eat a light meal before I go back to my hotel. Is there a café close by?

13) Everyone told me I must eat fish and chips while I'm in the UK. Where is the best place to go?

14) I'd like to go to a nice cheap restaurant. Where would you recommend?

15) How do I get there from here?

Example Conversations:
1)
Roberto: Do you usually go out for drinks after work?
Tom: During the week people are too busy. But on Fridays, everyone in the office goes to the bar across the road. Would you like to come along?
Roberto: Yes, I would like to join you.
Tom: OK. On Friday after work I'll come and find you.
Roberto: Thanks.

2)
Roberto: I'm thinking of going out for dinner tonight. Do you have any suggestions about restaurants?
Tom: How about I come with you? Do you like Chinese food?
Roberto: I love it. And it would be great if you came too.
Tom: Great. Let's invite a few of the others too. There's a new Chinese restaurant in the next street. We can go there.
Roberto: Sounds good!

Q: *What can I talk about in a restaurant or bar?*
Advice: The conversations will probably be about your country, your job or company. They might ask you what you do in your spare time. You can ask your new friends the same type of questions.

Don't talk about politics or religion. Don't ask people personal questions, such as age or if they are married. You can talk about the food you are eating and ask about local food you should try while you are visiting.

Here are some conversation starters:
1) How long have you been working here?
2) What do you do?
3) Where did you work before coming here?
4) How many people work for the company here?
5) What do you recommend?
6) This is a nice restaurant. Do you come here often?
7) Do you often go for drinks after work?
8) Are you interested in sports?
9) What local foods should I try while I am here?
10) What do you do in your spare time?

9. SAYING GOODBYE

Q. What is the polite way to say goodbye?

Advice: It is important to thank the managers in the office when you are saying goodbye. It is also good to say the trip was helpful, or useful. Here are some sentences you can use.

Example Sentences:
1) Thank you for having me over the past few days.
2) My trip here has been very useful/helpful.
3) You have given me some very good ideas.
4) I was very pleased to meet you and your staff.
5) Thank you for all your help/advice.
6) I will email you when I get back to my office.
7) My boss will be pleased. I have learned so much here.
8) I am looking forward to applying/using the systems/methods I have learnt here when I get back.
9) It was so useful to get to know the people here. Communication between our offices will be much easier,
10) I think we made good progress on combining our marketing strategies. They will be much more effective.

Example Conversation:
Roberto: I'm leaving tomorrow. Thank you for having me here over the past few days.
Karen: It has been a pleasure.
Roberto: My trip here has been very useful. You have given me

some very good ideas. Thank you for all your advice.

Karen: You're welcome. I'm glad it was useful. We learnt a lot from you too. Thank you for your interesting presentation.

Roberto: Thank you. I will email you when I get back to the Rome office.

Karen: OK, have a safe trip back home!

Q. Is it OK to ask to exchange social media information?

Advice: It is probably not a good idea to ask for social media information from the manager, or those you don't know very well. You can keep in contact with them by work email if necessary. If you become friendly with someone, then it is probably OK. Here are some sentences you can use.

Example Sentences:
1) Are you on Twitter/Facebook?
2) Can I send you a friend request?
3) What is your Skype/email address?
4) How can I keep in touch with you?
5) You can find me on Facebook.

Example Conversations:
1)
Roberto: I'm leaving tomorrow. It was great to meet you. Thanks for all your help.

Tom: No problem. Thank you too.

Roberto: Are you on Facebook?

Tom: Yes, I am.

Roberto: Can I send you a friend request?

Tom: Sure! Just search for Tom Farmer. You'll soon find me.

Roberto: OK, I'll do that when I get back.

Tom: Yeah, keep in touch! I hope I have the chance to visit the Rome office someday!

Roberto: I hope so too!

COFFEE BREAK

"I love going away on business. So far, I have been to London, Paris, and Frankfurt. The first time I visit the offices, I feel nervous, but I soon become friends with the people there. I keep in touch with some of them on Facebook. It is interesting to see their lives and their culture. When I visit the offices, we use English. The meetings are in English, and the presentations are in English, but I have started to learn French and German. I want to be able to give a presentation in French in the Paris office, and in German in the Frankfurt office. I want to surprise my friends there, so now, I am studying hard! Most of my friends here in Japan work for Japanese companies, and they don't have the chance to travel. I'm glad I chose an international company. Working for a global company has really changed my life."

Ms K.N. (38) Visits the UK, France and Germany frequently

"When going on business trips, I think English is important, but cultural knowledge is also important. Before I go, I read a lot on the Internet about the culture and customs of a country. For example, when I meet people, should I shake hands, or bow? Should I use their first names, or last names? Is it important to be punctual? What topics of conversation should I avoid? This research helps my trips to go smoothly. "

Mr G.P. (29) Visits Japan and Hong Kong frequently

10. CHECK OUT

Q. How can I get from the hotel to the airport?
Advice: Your hotel might have a shuttle bus. This might not run very often, so you should check at the front desk. If they do not have a shuttle bus, or if the time is not convenient, you can ask them to call you a taxi. Be sure to arrange transport to the airport the day or evening before you leave.

Example Sentences:
1) I'd like to check out.
2) Do you have a shuttle bus to the airport?
3) What time does the bus leave?
4) How often does the bus leave?
5) I need to be at the airport by 10:00am.
6) How long will it take to get to the airport?
7) How much is the bus?
8) Could you call me a taxi please?
9) How much is the taxi fare from here to the airport?
10) Could I have a receipt?

Example Conversations:
1)
Hotel staff: Good evening, Sir. Can I help you?
Roberto: Yes. I am checking out tomorrow morning. Do you have a shuttle bus to the airport?
Hotel staff: Yes, we do. It leaves every hour from the front doors.

The service starts at eight am.
Roberto: I need to be at the airport by ten am.
Hotel staff: In that case, it's better for you to take a taxi.
Roberto: Could you book/arrange a taxi for me please?
Hotel staff: Sure. I'll book one for you now. I will ask the taxi company to pick you up from here at seven thirty am.
Roberto: How much is the taxi fare from here to the airport?
Hotel staff: It's around thirty dollars.
Roberto: OK. Thank you. I will be in the lobby at seven fifteen am.

2)
Hotel staff: Good morning.
Roberto: Good morning. I'd like to check out.
Hotel staff: OK. Could I have your room card please?
Roberto: Here you are.
Hotel staff: Did you eat or drink anything from the mini bar in your room?
Roberto: No.
Hotel staff: Do you need a receipt?
Roberto: Yes, please.
Hotel staff: Just a moment. Here is your receipt. Thank you sir. I hope you enjoyed your stay.
Roberto: Yes, I did, thank you.
Hotel staff: Your taxi has arrived.
Roberto: Thank you.

THANK YOU

Thank you for reading Enjoy Your Business Trip. (Word count: 6,267) We hope you enjoyed it, and we hope you enjoy your business trip too!

If you would like to read more about business trips, please see our Level 1 graded reader "A Business Trip to New York".

If you would like to read more graded readers, please visit our website http://www.italkyoutalk.com

Other Level 3 graded readers include
A Dangerous Weekend
A Holiday to Remember
Akiko and Amy Part 1
Akiko and Amy Part 2
Akiko and Amy Part 3
Be My Valentine
Different Seas
Enjoy Your Homestay
I Need a Friend
Old Jack's Ghost Stories from England (1)
Old Jack's Ghost Stories from England (2)
Old Jack's Ghost Stories from Ireland
Old Jack's Ghost Stories from Japan
Old Jack's Ghost Stories from Scotland

Old Jack's Ghost Stories from Wales
Party Time!
Stories for Christmas
The Curse
Together Again
Who is Holly?

ABOUT THE AUTHOR

I Talk You Talk Press is a Japan-based publisher of language textbooks, graded readers and language learning/teaching resources.

Our team is made up of highly experienced language teachers and translators, who have all studied at least one additional language to an advanced level.

This experience enables us to design our materials from the perspective of both the teacher and the learner. We consult with both teachers and language learners when designing our textbooks and graded readers, and test our materials extensively in the classroom before publication.

We are a fast-growing press, and currently publish graded readers for learners of English. We publish new graded readers monthly.

www.ingramcontent.com/pod-product-compliance
Lightning Source LLC
Chambersburg PA
CBHW032005060426
42449CB00031B/806